Yorkshire Crabs

F. Mary Callan

Stairwell Books //

Published by Stairwell Books
161 Lowther Street
York, YO31 7LZ

www.stairwellbooks.co.uk
@stairwellbooks

Yorkshire Crabs © 2023 Mary Callan and Stairwell Books

All rights reserved. No part of this publication may be reproduced, stored in or introduced into a retrieval system, or transmitted, in any form, or by any means (electronic, mechanical, photocopying, recording, e-book or otherwise) without the prior written permission of the author or publisher.

The moral rights of the author have been asserted.

ISBN: 978-1-913432-79-9

In gratitude to my parents, Tony and Morrie Callan

Table of Contents

Yorkshire Crabs	1
Vin Garbutt	2
River Tyne, Reclaimed	3
Whitby Sea Defences	4
Red Clay	5
Trajectory	6
Embers	7
York's Nuclear Bunker	8
Housing Estate	9
Tombstone Alley	10
SVB Collapse	11
DR Congo	12
Deforestation	13
Hyrax (Lebanon, Israel, Syria)	14
Grey Squirrels, UK	15
Winter Sunset	16
Sunrise	17
Holgate Windmill, York	18
Acomb Water Tower, York	19
After the Frost	20
Spring Pond	21
Garden Ponds	22
Snails	23
Pigeons	24
Pigeon Families	25
February Blitz	26
Wild Vetch	27
The Yorkshire Esk	28
Yorkshire Shepherds	29
Hole of Horcum	30
Farndale in Spring	31
Eco Choices	32
Bittercress	33

Drumbeat	34
Every Species Dreams of Domination	35
Below the Ramparts	37
Peacock Butterflies on Mauve	38
Hyacinths' Progress	39
Campanula	40
Another Rascal	41
Welcome? – or Not?	42
Flower-Arranger	43
Alliums	44
Neighbours	45
Wonder	46
Pause	47
Hope	48
Editor	49

Yorkshire Crabs

The beach is empty now;
No more dead crabs and lobsters
In stinking heaps;
All gone, all gone.
Eighteen months of pleading with Westminster,
"There really is a problem.
This needs fixing."
"What problem?
All gone."
Empty beaches too
Round Italy and Greece and Spain,
And Kent,
No more exhausted migrants,
Until the next tide,
And the next landings,
Or the next delivery of human flotsam.
"There really is a problem.
This needs fixing."
"Not our problem.
Don't look now.
Don't look till the beaches are empty.
See!
No problem!

Vin Garbutt

A troubadour might sing of trouble
And open up our eyes.
He sings to help our hearts to grieve.
He sings to wake the wise.
Oh, Vin, should'st thou be living at this hour!
You sang of pollution, "orange, violet and grey,"
And longed for clean skies and clean water,
Sickened by the "amber Tees bay."
Are you turning in your grave,
That, although the industry has gone,
And the jobs have gone,
And meaning and purpose and heart,
Yes, heart,
Have been ripped out of the community,
As if that wasn't enough,
Under the clean sky and clean water, at last,
The powers-that-be have dredged up,
Literally dredged up,
And they won't even admit it,
Old, old seabed dumps,
That had settled, doing no harm to anybody,
And the death and destruction on the seabed is horrendous,
Littering the beaches,
And they still won't admit it.

River Tyne, Reclaimed

"Well, the river's still in the same place,"
Said my brother, as we loitered,
Waiting for a funeral,
"But not much else."
There used to be houses here,
Terrace houses, roomy and elegant,
Sturdy and strong,
Nothing wrong with them,
Demolished because unneeded;
Because the river, in its same place,
Is not the same river,
Silver, serene, unbelievably clean,
Like an old person parked in a care home.
Designer flats gaze over its tranquil flow,
Where fishermen, seamen, hustlers of all kinds,
Among ropes and noise and ordered activity,
Earned a living, decades ago.
All the bustle of the working river,
Clang of shipyards,
Ferries, tugs, the cruise ships to Norway, the whaler,
Busy fish quay, rocking boats, patter of the
auctioneer,
Towering derricks and
Dust from loading coal,
Nothing remains.
Only the clean, shining, *empty* river
In the same place.

Whitby Sea Defences

There are holes in the ramparts.
During my walk on the beach
I collect a thin black flake,
Smooth and slender in my palm,
With a neat round hole like a knot-hole,
Really intriguing, almost an artefact.
Others are scattered along the sand,
Artlessly, carelessly, swished around by tides.
What are those intruders,
Those black, angular rocks
Dumped where the cliff lowers
And is vulnerable?
Fetched from Norway, do they say?
And dumped here, strategically,
To defend our retreating coastline?
Well, how can it work?
The thing's riddled with holes already.

Red Clay

Wet walk along the Whitby coast,
One rainy day,
Daddy and two little girls.
We stopped at a muddy gully.
"Can you model with it?" asked my dad,
Kneading red mud in his hands,
Redness like juice over his fingers,
As workmen paused on their spades.
"Will it take a firing?"
"Just take some and try it."
Just like the chunks of clay on the beach
I'd been told not to touch.
"They'll make you all muddy."
Weeks later, at home, we modelled it.
I think dad made a mug or a cup.
It was never good for firing,
We only had the kitchen oven.
Decades later,
I shape some people in pottery class
And feel the joy of creation.

Trajectory

Is there an OFF switch?
Can we abort the descent?
Is doom negotiable?
Hurtling downwards?
Or onwards?

Perhaps, Just as x^2 times y^2
Can swing the parabola
And loop the downward slope upwards,
Or the downhill skier
Be launched skyward by an intervening, friendly ramp,
Perhaps for our world too,
Redemption looms, recovery, restoration,
–- Or perhaps not.

Embers

We are an old civilisation.
We sit like witches round a dying fire,
Poking the embers for a final flicker.
See! See! How an orange flame jumps,
Sudden and swift,
And again!
And dies.
Nothing,
So jab again.

Rome came to this,
Civilisation faltering,
Little wars all round,
Crumbling infrastructure,
Plague, plague, plague,
Destitution and hunger,
The same enemies gathering around our fire.

Will the world re-knit itself, as then,
Emerge in new forms, new values,
Like weeds emerging, spreading, evolving,
Proving useful,
The restart for a new world?
Around the embers,
We dream. ✎

York's Nuclear Bunker

200 metres from my flat,
Sign-posted now,
Still hidden,
Is York's biggest relic of the Cold War,
The nuclear bunker,
Constructed secretly, under a rocky hill,
Never used.
When exactly was it built?
50s or 60s?
I don't know.
I ought to visit it,
Do the tourist thing, and find out more.
But I remember clearly,
The 60s, and all that.
We were sure we wouldn't see 1970.
That date was unthinkable.
We'd be wiped out well before then.
– All the worry over Strontium-90.
—- *You*'ve never heard of it!
– Nothing much worries me now.

Housing Estate

A garden suburb forty years ago,
1930s semis,
And a post-war council estate beside it,
Well-built, robust and prosperous;
Gardens all round, generous,
Rose bushes in front,
Fruit and veg in back.
Gradually a few designer gardens appeared,
With tricky brickwork, worth a second glance,
– Of course, the horticulture graduates! –
But now, each house is an island
In a carpark, flagged, hard-cored and sterile;
Such prosperity,
Two cars where every lawn once was,
Or three, or even five;
But who can calculate the cost
Of no more hedgehogs,
No more butterflies,
Foxes roaming further, hungrier,
And the rain, rain, rain
That drum, drum, drums
On the hard harsh arid concrete,
And gurgles away too fast
Along overflowing gutters,
For floods downstream?

Tombstone Alley

The high street is empty and boarded up
Like a row of graves,
Like the aisle of a cemetery.
We trudge past dead lives,
Gaps, vacancies,
A past that's gone,
No future.
Asset-stripped,
Woolworth's, Littlewoods, BHS, and more,
As though the ground has been pulled from under them,
And the river can rise from behind
And float them away.
The finance has flowed into off-shore bank accounts,
Fattened and often forgotten.
Most of it will never emerge again,
Hoarded ad infinitem,
Doing nothing;
Boarded up shops and hoarded up riches;

And people have nowhere to shop,
Nor money to buy.

SVB Collapse

It's all in the mind.
Another banking collapse sweeps out,
Threatening the world;
Loans, out on a limb, too risky,
Threatening to topple,
Threatening a tsunami
Throughout the global invisible world.
I picture waves, towering ocean waves,
Waves to surf on or be drowned by
And rolled up on the beach,
No longer breathing.
Is it even real, this finance?
Was it ever real?
Were these deals and loans
All in the minds,
The fertile mental ant-heaps of human brains
And human ingenuity;
Potential wealth, currency with no foundation;
I see the wave, is it toppling?
Worldwide undertakings, all invisible;
The 'net, the firewalls, the bugs and viruses,
The shields, the sneaky spies and malware,
The hackers and the 'good guys';
Our whole world ruled and shaken
By invisible realities,
All in the minds;
How unreal! ⁄⁄

DR Congo

What is most precious?
Lives are being lost here,
Daily,
Hourly,
As desperate humans scrabble
For diamonds,
or silver,
or the rare earths needed for communication;
Swarming and tunnelling like ants,
Scuffling and slipping;
Teamwork?
No!
Even the ants could teach them.
Here is desperation,
"Every man for himself."
Poverty teaches us all to grovel,
Grubbing in the ground;
Poverty, despoiling and fragmenting the human tribe,
While the millionaires laugh.

Deforestation

Lives are being lost here.
The jungle is betrayed,
Not for its own sake,
Not for timber, or fruit,
Or even farmland.
The very earth itself
Is stolen, torn apart, raped and stripped,
Stripped and raped,
For greed, big and small.
Desperate diggers,
With spades,
Or even without;
No income,
No trade or job or any future,
Dig for a dream,
Even the tiniest diamond.

Behind the scenes,
The fat-cats dream as well,
To dominate, exterminate,
Eliminate the rival,
Float to the top,
Whatever the turmoil.

Hyrax (Lebanon, Israel, Syria)

You're a success story,
Rock rabbits, hyrax, relative of elephants,
– Your shaggy coats are more like mammoths' –
I couldn't get your photo.
You hardly showed up to the camera,
So late in the dusk,
Though my mere human eyes could see you,
All six of you, grey against grey.
I really must congratulate you,
There you go, spreading and multiplying,
In a war zone.
Where humans are fleeing
And the landscape is devastated,
You are flourishing.
Rock rabbits, four times as numerous,
Among shattered concrete,
21st century rocks, utterly at home.
That's not the only success.
If you're there, you're not alone.
You're a sign that vegetation is flourishing.
Nature is unvanquished.
She's holding on,
And there'll be a world to return to.

Grey Squirrels, UK

You say I don't belong, despite the grace
With which I seem to float from tree to tree,
Tail, spread like a sail, and paws extended,
I scamper, pause, and skip. Just let me be.
Is it my fault your red squirrel can't compete?
Find them a new home. Have they tried Norway?
I'm sure they'd love it. *And* they hibernate.
What could be more suited? Better than your way.
There'll be a reason why we flourish in exile.
One hundred and fifty years, we're everywhere.
It's just so lovely here. You know we're pretty,
Pretty adorable! Don't pretend you don't care.
And we're far smaller than the hippos,
Cluttering rivers in Colombia;
And we might be useful someday,
Recolonising our old home,
Like endangered species returned to the wild;
Think of Père David's deer in China.
You never know when we'll be needed.
Life's very fragile, You know it, child.

Winter Sunset

The sun is setting over Hobmoor,
A winter sunset, slow and chill.
The glowing orange ball
Slithers above a slice of cloud,
Grey, lying in wait.
Higher clouds
Are underlit with tangerine.
The darkening turf,
Three-quarters surrendered to night,
Hugs the last sparkle, like gauze,
Like a fallen scarf.
I gather its light round my feet,
hurrying to the exit.
Sixteen hours till sunrise.
I won't be here.
Busy days will swallow me.
Only this early sunset,
Low-lit and lingering,
Is mine to keep.

Sunrise

Dawn, in sweet sugar pink,
I see you on Facebook.
Unpredictable, we can't reserve a ticket.
Through weeks of grey, I've been waiting,
Off and on,
But not today;
And today, you made a show,
Ethereal,
Undefinable,
Utterly fairy pink.
Thank goodness for Facebook,
Where friends can show me what I've missed.
The show will go on,
Tantalisingly,
'Will she? Won't she?
'This week? Next week? Sometime?. .''
But never 'Never.'
Dawn, Aurora,
Winsome pink or angry scarlet,
Or grey-as-nothing risings
− You have your bad hair days,
Just like the rest of us, −
But you haven't failed us yet.

Holgate Windmill, York

Your sails are still today,
Shining white in the sunshine.
"How futile!" I thought, when they rebuilt you.
"What a waste of cash,
And what a waste of a romantic ruin,
An authentic, unspoilt, heap of stone."
But during Lockdown,
With flour shortages and panic-buying,
The queue, socially-distanced,
Stretched along the avenue,
Waiting patiently,
Each to buy a little bag of flour.
Medieval millers
Watch from their eternal rest
And rub their hands with glee.

Acomb Water Tower, York

You are what you are,
With no pretence,
Pillars of concrete and the water tank,
Just a big barrel, a huge one, on legs,
And mains water pipes up and down.
I hope you're a listed building.
You deserve it,
In your fading, historic green paint.
Redundancy wasn't your fault.
Still perfectly functional.
It's the bureaucrats and all their paperwork.
You know what they're like.
"No, that door's not wide enough,
Nor high enough.
You can't count on fitting a man through there.
We're bigger nowadays.
What if he got stuck?"
"It's never happened."
"No, but it says here, What if it might?"
No accessibility for maintenance.
Tower condemned and redundant.
Monument to an earlier, slimmer age,
And to Health & Safety and all its
(insert your own adjective of choice)
Bureaucracy. ⁄⁄

After the Frost

Water is streaming down our road,
Clear and sparkling,
Chattering and chuckling like a mountain stream,
Happy and free.
Twenty days have flushed the gutter clean,
Crystal-clean, and grey as mountain pebbles.
The water's song,
The glint of sun,
The clarity,
All speak to me of mountain walks,
Long strides in the fresh air,
A joyful climb.
Beautiful clear water,
Yorkshire's best,
Yorkshire Water's best,
The endless happy song,
All wasted down the gutter,
Profligate clarity,
One of ten bursts fountaining in our half-kilometre,
Neglected infrastructure;
A force unharnessed,
Purity, wasted.

Spring Pond

How many million years
To form the eyes that look out of the water
So trustingly?
Frogs, in pairs, conjugal happiness,
Clinging, grey in the grey pond,
Where life begins again
Each year.

Do I mean anything to you,
Grey bulging eyes,
As my shadow falls across the water,
And moves, as I stroll,
Seeking the best angle,
Trying to avoid the dazzle on the water,
To see you better,
Aside from my reflection?
Mesmerised, enchanted, rapt, intrigued
By the new emerging lives
Under grey water.

Garden Ponds

"Did you see the heron?
Are you sure it was the culprit?"
"Yes, I saw the heron,
Grey and fat and eating my pond's little fish."
It's a lovely pond,
Planned and arranged with care,
Installed by professionals,
To encourage wildlife,
And promote a varied ecology.
The trees leaning over it are waiting for leaves.
Wisps of green algae trail in the water,
Too rich in nutrients.
No other life
Since the heron's final visit.
A few gardens closer,
Tucked deep under an evergreen,
The re-purposed babybath,
Filled with rainwater,
Is heaving with life,
Frogs bob in the healthy green duckweed.
Does the heron know it's here?
Shall I carry some frogspawn along to the other?
And the heron? Friend or foe?
Shall we look for an eagle to deal with it?
Whose side are we on?

Snails

Wet drive is alive in the rainy dark,
Alive in the pattering rain.
The snails advance,
Each two-pronged head stretched,
Exploring eagerly,
Sharing the charge.
Daytime concrete was dead,
Still as a tomb,
But now, surprise,
The reflected light shows me a world in movement,
A world of determination,
of journeys and exploration;
No idle wanderings,
They're set for a destination;

And tomorrow, after the rain,
The drive will be dead again.

Pigeons

Thanks to the pigeons,
No need to weed the moss out of the cracks.
They scour the courtyard,
Ripping the moss from between the setts.
They have paid special attention to the sill of my front door,
Where my accessible flat
Has no step to repel the dust,
So moss thought it could make a home.
No!
Thanks to the pigeons,
The doorsill is stripped and clean.

At least mine's the ground floor flat.
The pigeons' activities under the solar panels
Are not my problem.

Pigeon Families

Pigeons believe in the future.
On an untidy balcony
Overlooking the river
And the morning sun,
They've shuffled a few twigs together,
And now there's a pure white egg,
Just one.
Patiently, the parents keep it warm.
Devotedly, the parents feed that chick.
Not many weeks, it's almost as big as they are,
And ready to fly.
So the parents do it again.
One egg, a single chick, two doting parents,
That's pigeon family life,
Perhaps two months in total,
And start again.
This time, it's twins.
The soft-hearted balcony owner
Admits, "I can't bear to tidy up
And sweep them away."
My side of the city,
The cooing under the solar-panels is deafening.
I see occasional shards of fallen egg-shell,
Perfectly white.

February Blitz

"Both the apple trees?"
"Both the apple trees!"
Every tree and shrub sheared off,
Felled and cleared and the earth left bare,
In February blitz.
For why?
To forestall all the protections
And paperwork
That might hamper development.
Clear everything before the 1st of March.
There'll be no survey for nesting birds.
The date that should have protected them
Just made destruction more urgent.
Developers may not begin for months yet,
The whole nesting season might have passed
successfully,
Songs and happy families,
Undisturbed,
Without this deadly deadline.
Hah! Already, the 1st of April,
Beside the wall,
Willow shoots are budding,
Two feet high.
They think they've merely been coppiced.

Wild Vetch

Sky-blue vetch, such precious, sapphire blue.
Such memories from childhood.
I ran to pick a sprig from the cliff's edge.
An anxious voice, a parent in alarm, called me back.
"Never run to the edge of the cliff like that.
You can't see. It's been undercut, ready to fall."
Did I pick the vetch, or was I called back too quickly?
Always an avid gatherer, always reckless.
Years in exile from that sapphire blue.
Years of other vetches,
Making do
With faded purple,
Outlandish, unexpected, glorious sunny yellow,
Sexy magenta.
That sky-blue, sapphire blue, haunts me still,
Elusive,
And a memory of life spared,
And a worried parent's gentle explanation,
Over the overhang.

The Yorkshire Esk

The little river valley is like a half-open eye,
Blink, and you'll miss it,
But here is the real truth,
Mixed deciduous woodland,
English native trees,
Rustling with native flora and fauna;

Tucked down from the moors,
– So much more famous,
With their imperial purple
One month each year,
But fake, really,
Only maintained for the convenience and the fame,
Maintained for the grouse-shooting;
For centuries, stripped and laid bare
By the mining,
Lead-mining, iron-mining, arsenic, potash, silver,
You name it, they've mined it,
And kept bare ever since
For August's purple moment
And the grouse.

Yorkshire Shepherds

Seventy years ago
I welcomed their steady stroll,
A farmer and his teenage son
Leading three hundred sheep
Along the moor road,
Last day of the wettest August.
Three miles they'd tramped,
Patient and slow,
Gathered the flock and walked them
Here, to be dipped.
They knew their value:
Wool would fetch its price
And so would lamb, young lamb,
A treat, affordable to some.
The teenager worked at the dipping-trough,
Plunging the sheep.
"Not this old tup," said his father,
"He's too strong for thee. Leave him to us,
And mind the horns."
Seventy years on
The sheep travel by wagon,
Three tiers of stock, patient, hardly bleating.
Have they a value?
Wool can't reach its price;
Roast lamb is a luxury undreamed of,
And farmers go bankrupt. ⁄⁄

Hole of Horcum

"They would stop in the Hole of Horcum
And pick bilberries
And bring us bowls full."
My mum was reminiscing
About her cousins' summer journeys
Across the moors, pre-WWII.
I picture the Hole of Horcum,
Where our dad slithered down a path,
Laughing, among the bracken;
Topology almost perfect,
Another 'Devil's Punchbowl,'
Drained by its little beck.
Not many bilberries now,
Their midget shrubs and tiny leaves,
And berries, better than blueberries.
The green tide of bracken swishes up the slopes,
Swallowing everything, wave over wave.
Where did you come from, you tough invader?
How can we tackle you?
You're quite graceful in your own way,
Tall and green, frondy and curly,
Stooping over us like a doting nanny.
A little of you would be quite ornamental,
But enough's enough!

Farndale in Spring

"Are there still coach trips to visit the daffodils?"
My children's father hated crowds.
We went when the valley was empty,
Later in spring,
The turf sprinkled with thistles,
Low, lying in wait.
No crowds,
Just springy turf and friendly sunshine,
A few sheep, far away, ignoring us.
Nothing of interest except the thistles,
"Ouch, here's another one,"
Smelling sweetly of honey;
Butterflies landing here and there,
Fluttering and pausing, enjoying a sip;
Visiting insects hovering,
Constantly, quietly buzzing
On that sleepy afternoon.
Such a mischievous, prickly plant,
So well-hidden, well-trodden.
Fragrant with honey.

Eco Choices

'What can I do? What can I do?'
Should I have left the thistles?
Would they have done a better job
Of welcoming the bees?
Their honey softness,
Their heavy sway in summer warmth,
The music as their court assembles,
So many happy clients,
Honey-filled and happy,
Roaming the armoury.
Those swords are needed,
Six-inch or six-foot spikes
Of bristling pricks
Deter us humans,
But don't repel the clients,
Ferrying gold, at last,
To distant hives.
But they'll be just as happy with cosmos.

Bittercress

So many local weeds are new to me.
I've learned a lot of names in forty years.
Did people eat you? Were you a salad green?
Careful inspection shows a family likeness
To watercress,
The same ladder of leaves,
In miniature, or is that just your youth?
I haven't tolerated any further growth.
Same lovely glossy green as watercress,
Same tuft of clean white flowers,
Cross-shaped, like so much edible stuff,
Or poisonous too.
I'd better be careful.
Did my parents know you?
Did you grow wild as close to the coast?
Or am I breaking new ground,
Learning your name,
And considering whether to nibble,
And at what cost?

Drumbeat

It's the drum, drum, drumbeat to nothing,
Never been so close before;
The drum, drum, drum beat that's hollow,
Loudest at the empty door;

The door of despair and "So what?"
The shrug and the empty hands;
The beat that repeats to the empty air
And whistles on the clueless winds.

But here, it has lifted my pavement
And opened my earth to the sky.
New sunflowers nod to the neighbours.
There's green where it was paved and dry.

There's a buzz, buzz, buzz among the yellow.
There are ladybirds under the leaves.
The old pests are chomp, chomp, chomping
Their new chance, in a world that grieves.

Every Species Dreams of Domination

Photos in my memory –
Forty years ago,
A ten-foot stretch of honesty,
Purple wall guarding the lawn,
Solid and royal, all through May
Imperial parade,
Spring triumph;

Fifteen years ago, a frame of blue
Like fallen sky,
Forget-me-nots in millions,
Crowding,
Luminous,
Around the lawn.

From tumbled compost,
Sunflowers rose like an army,
Mounting gold,
Satellite dishes with yellow frills,
High on selfie-sticks,
Drilled to follow the sun across the sky.

And do you remember the noughties?
A decade or dozen years,
Of lavateras?
Mallow bushes, everywhere, self-sown,
Six-foot shrubs in pink or mauve or white or stripy,
Waving in the wind at every garden's end.
Where are they now?

Arums in early summer
On high, in black-and-white,
Sweet fragrance of the white,
Rotten stench of the black,
Guess which the hoverflies love most?

Late summer explodes in orange,
Vivid electric orange
Of chinese lanterns everywhere,
Drooping, lounging, erect,
Swags of perfect lanterns;
From the passionflower,
Pendant orange grenadillas;
On stinking iris,
Open pods of orange seeds,
Radiating like wind turbines, in threesomes;
But chinese lanterns will overwhelm them all.

September, orange!
October, orange!
November, still brilliant shining orange
Among the brittle desiccated foliage.
December, waiting to move house,
I gather orange seeds, three kinds,
To plant them all in pots,
And spread the glow.

Every species is sure
The planet is theirs to own,
Theirs alone.
Till the next species grabs a turn. ⁄⁄

Below the Ramparts

There are patches where the daffodils can't bloom
In the shade of the cherry trees;
Circles of green bereft of gold;
A bruise on springtime's face;
A nagging vacancy
Of green gloom,
Despite the lightsome afternoon.
We've been robbed here,
While daffodils flaunt themselves all round.
One tree already swagged in pink,
Heavy chunks of blossom bending the boughs
Swaying their ponderous dance,
Priming the parade
Behind the bus-stops.
Van Gogh, floating pink,
Happy, frothing pink,
Is on its way,
But not ethereal yet,
To be released upon the breeze,
With task complete,
And fill the ground like snow
In three weeks' time,
Even scattering onto the dull green;
Each circle shadow still reminding us
How one good thing deprives us of another ⁄⁄

Peacock Butterflies on Mauve

Where are the peacocks of yesteryear?
Where is the cloud of eyes
That hovered around the buddleia,
Peacock butterflies, thronging the purple fronds
In early 90s summers?
A species I'd never seen before,
So numerous,
For just a few years.
And red admirals, at least one summer,
Was it before or after?
Not as long.
And recently,
Brimstones,
Lesser blues,
And both sizes of tortoiseshell.
But where is it all leading?
Is Nature taking us
Forwards or Backwards? ⁄⁄

Hyacinths' Progress

I have to admit,
That blue is gentian blue,
Lurking under the shrubbery
In a little front garden.
Eight glamorous hyacinths
In that lovely glowing blue,
Yes! Gentian blue!
No-one planted them
Except the first one.
They've made their own progress,
Neglected, unnoticed,
Left to 'do their own thing'
Under the bushes.
Nature always has another card to play,
Unexpected,
Pulled from behind our backs.
These hyacinths spread,
Slowly, secretly,
Out of control.
The planet is not finished yet.

Campanula

For weeks in early summer
Creeping campanula escapes the gardens,
Piling its blue stars everywhere;
Flooding under the gate and up the steps,
Outlining every flagstone on the path,
Trailing along to the neighbours,
Climbing the walls,
Everywhere, heaps of shining green and gentle blue,
Spreading, unstoppable, unless you're ruthless,
And who would want to be?
The wanderer is so pretty.
Sometimes a partner in crime,
Yellow corydalis,
Or greater celandine,
Accompanies it on its rambles,
Yellow and blue,
Yellow and blue,
Tufty yellow and fluid blue.
Nature is never vanquished.

Another Rascal

There's buddleia against the wall, in every crack,
Fountaining mauve and purple, white and ochre.
In every crevice the streets are under attack.
The gutter is sprouting sprigs. The compost heap
Is ambushed and surrounded.
Paving stones rise up in surrender,
Too many roots going under.
The fence is yielding.
Planks are leaning and split.
Brickwork is cracking, roots reaching out of it.
The whole built world is open to invasion.
Who held sway before you?
And who fed the butterflies who throng you now?
Bandit king!
Gorgeous, unstoppable, butterfly-laden,
Sweet honey-scented, narcotic, addictive,
Glorious, glamorous, opportunistic,
Successful adventurer,
Invader, settler, coloniser,
You!

Welcome? – or Not?

"Have you checked if they're edible?"
I asked my neighbour,
As she heaved some brown fungi out of the lawn,
And from under the silver birches,
And from among the irises,
And from under the appletree,
Plump brown boletus,
(Looking like horse manure,
But a different smell.)
"They might be very expensive.
It's worth checking."
"Not interested," she replied, lifting the lid
And dumping them into the compost bin.
"Not interested. I don't care."
In my own garden, my previous one,
The perfect white edible mushrooms
Hiding under the leylandii hedge
Were delicious.
Edible? Yes, I checked.
Even better
if I'd washed off the sand more thoroughly.

In the compost bin,
The bolete are making plans.

Flower-Arranger

Pentecost in York minster,
Crimson dahlias and yellow gladioli,
Raised in displays to hold our gaze
Eight feet high,
Like fire from heaven.

Her bright brown eyes meet mine.
Her enthusiasm is infectious.
"It was an accidental hobby.
The cake-decorating class was full.
We booked into flower-arranging.
I was hooked.
I couldn't have done it without my hubby.
He carried the deliveries.
He filled the buckets and kept the flowers fresh."

Some arrangers' work is breath-taking,
Like a new creation,
Fresh imagination,
When we look at an arrangement and gasp,
Like Eve, walking in the garden of Eden,
Among flowers fresh from the mind of the Creator.

Alliums

The shadows on my wall are very subtle,
Gentle grey against the gentle cream
Of softened sunlight, reflected off a car,
Such purity and clarity,
Perfect points of starry allium,
Last year's seedheads,
The dried-out ball I treasure.
Memories
Of mauve globes of alliums,
Poised like lanterns held on sticks,
Spheres of six-petalled flowers,
Each in place, forming the sphere,
Dancing above the flowerbed,
While hoverflies hover.
A mathematician's delight
At the ball's structure,
Then the starry six-pronged seedheads,
And the capsule, holding three fat seeds,
Now shadowed onto the wall.
And I remember
The charred outlines onto a wall in Nagasaki
And Hiroshima,
And wonder
What shadow will I leave?

Neighbours

Covid left five empty beds
In my little road.
Two were merciful:
Long, gentle lives, well lived.
Some were wrenched, untimely,
"Such a gap."
One home remains a mausoleum
With dead plants at the door, reproachful.
We patch things up.
One of our over-nineties,
Pushing her walking-aid up the road,
Tells me, "I get visitors.
Sid comes across every Thursday."
I am glad to learn
That friendly man, widowed now,
Has company on Thursdays.
His wife was a joy to all,
A talented seamstress,
Hub of a talented team,
Convenor of a bustling coffee-morning.
The cakes were 'out-of-this-world!'
Now, so is she.
We miss her.
We patch things up. ✎

Wonder

Streams flowed
And Adam stood with Eve
As a world happened.
Under the budding, leafing trees
They dug and tilled the soil,
Sowed seed
And harvested,
Tamed wildlife,
Tended and shepherded,
All without tuition.
Till, now,
The planet groans under concrete;
Rivers stink with sewage;
Humankind despise, discard each other.
Can we restore
The beauty of a moment,
Forget-me-nots,
A butterfly,
A toddler, happy on unsteady legs,
And catch our breath
In wonder?

Pause

Sometimes
Eternity is just a step away.
Among the 1930s redbrick semis
Here, a longer garden
Halts me completely,
Timeless.
How can I embrace
The peace beyond peace that arrests me here?
Is it the serenity of centuries
Between the trimmed cypresses?
The proportions of the long rectangular pond,
And the flagstone path around it, severe and bare?
The ebony gleam of the still water?
Its shining calm?
The stately authority of the wandering goldfish?
Or the gentle prettiness of the low-key flowerbeds?
Here, eternity grips me.
Whether I move or stay,
It holds me still. ✎

Hope

I have seen the future,
A steep green valley in the kingdom of Jordan.
"All it took was that little dam," says our guide,
Looking down proudly on the pattern of fields,
Orchards, a few houses.
"And what was most unexpected,
The nomads have moved in.
They abandoned their wandering
And are joining in:
Settled lives, like everyone else.
Their children are going to school.
It's a win for everyone."
Five minutes behind us
Stretches the desert,
Hundreds of miles,
Rocks and shingle, dry as bone;
Below us, the future,
A green jigsaw of new life,
New lives.
Sahara! Here we come!
To undo the ravages of centuries,
Slowly, slowly restore the missing water
Or tame the floods.
Make Sahara green again,
Re-storation after de-forestation.
Timbuktu *can* be relieved.

Editor

Trim the flowery ones.
Ramp up the pain.
Less sunshine, lots more rain.
They won't do anything till they're feeling guilty.
Just remind them, the planet's filthy.
It all needs cleaning and turning green.
Paint them a future that's all pristine.
But what about Alexander Fleming
Who wouldn't have noticed penicillin
If his lab dishes had been clean instead of neglected,
A benefit no-one suspected?
So, be merciful to the muck
And merciful to each other.
The planet will survive.
It's survived before.
Just stop being greedy,
And stop being lazy,
And look after human beings,
The most wonderful species on the planet,
And make sure
We're part of the cure!

About the Author

(Frances) Mary Callan was born in Whitby and grew up near Tynemouth. She obtained a B.A(Hons) in French and Latin at the university of Newcastle-upon-Tyne. Always a poetry-lover, it was not till her late forties, advised to find a hobby, that Mary stumbled into writing, dramatic monologues at first, and then rhyming poetry, fairy tales and short fiction.

2013-19 Mary performed her one-woman shows at the Edinburgh Fringe, BLAZING GRANNIES Bible drama and SPARKLING GRANNY new legends and fairy tales. Her newest show is WITH A DOG AND AN ANGEL, a musical based on the Story of Tobias.

The YORKSHIRE CRABS sequence of rhetorical poetry is a new venture for Mary. Always reluctant to depress her audience, Mary hopes this frank, sometimes humorous, account of our world, in all its beauty and problems, will encourage us in our efforts to care for it and each other.

Mary's published work includes
CHRISTMAS PATCHWORK, 'live reports from Bethlehem' pub. Sessions of York, 1999
SIDE DOOR INTO THE GOSPEL, self-published, 2016
OUT OF THE DREAMING DARK, poems on the Seven Days of Creation, pub. Stairwell books, 2020
THE ANURAN SAGA fairy tales, pub. Pegasus-Nightingale books, 2023

Visit Mary's website: www.notsodeadpoet.com

Other anthologies and collections available from Stairwell Books

The Estuary and the Sea	Jennifer Keevill
In | Between	Angela Arnold
Quiet Flows the Hull	Clint Wastling
Lunch on a Green Ledge	Stella Davis
there is an england	Harry Gallagher
Iconic Tattoo	Richard Harries
Fatherhood	CS Fuqua
Herdsmenization	Ngozi Olivia Osuoha
On the Other Side of the Beach, Light	Daniel Skyle
Words from a Distance	Ed. Amina Alyal, Judi Sissons
Fractured	Shannon O'Neill
Unknown	Anna Rose James, Elizabeth Chadwick Pywell
When We Wake We Think We're Whalers from Eden	Bob Beagrie
Awakening	Richard Harries
Starspin	Graehame Barrasford Young
Out of the Dreaming Dark	Mary Callan
A Stray Dog, Following	Greg Quiery
Blue Saxophone	Rosemary Palmeira
Steel Tipped Snowflakes 1	Izzy Rhiannon Jones, Becca Miles, Laura Voivodeship
Where the Hares Are	John Gilham
The Glass King	Gary Allen
A Thing of Beauty Is a Joy Forever	Don Walls
Gooseberries	Val Horner
Poetry for the Newly Single 40 Something	Maria Stephenson
Northern Lights	Harry Gallagher
Nothing Is Meant to be Broken	Mark Connors
Heading for the Hills	Gillian Byrom-Smith
More Exhibitionism	Ed. Glen Taylor
The Beggars of York	Don Walls
Lodestone	Hannah Stone
Unsettled Accounts	Tony Lucas
Learning to Breathe	John Gilham
New Crops from Old Fields	Ed. Oz Hardwick
The Ordinariness of Parrots	Amina Alyal

For further information please contact rose@stairwellbooks.com

www.stairwellbooks.co.uk
@stairwellbooks